I CAN MAKE

MY OWN ACCESSORIES

Easy-to-follow patterns to make
and customize fashion accessories

Thames & Hudson

I CAN MAKE

MY OWN ACCESSORIES

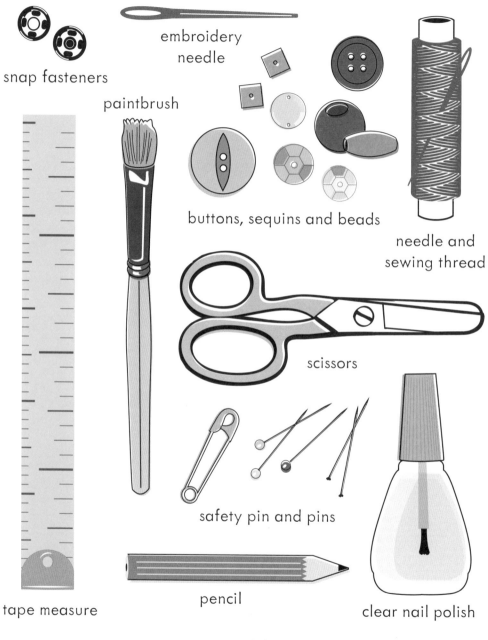

snap fasteners

embroidery needle

paintbrush

buttons, sequins and beads

needle and sewing thread

scissors

tape measure

safety pin and pins

pencil

clear nail polish

essential kit

let's make

Follow the simple step-by-step instructions in this book to make stylish accessories to wear and to give to your friends and family.

Before you start, go to page 170 to learn tips and techniques that you will use to make your accessories.

On pages 160–69 there are lots of ideas for how to design and customize your own creations, using the same materials and techniques as the projects in this book.

Why not start collecting fabric scraps, buttons and ribbons to make your accessories? Try creating different looks by using all sorts of colors and patterns.

remember
Always point needles and pins away from you. If you can't cut your fabric with rounded scissors, ask a grown-up to help you use some sharper ones.

a lips brooch

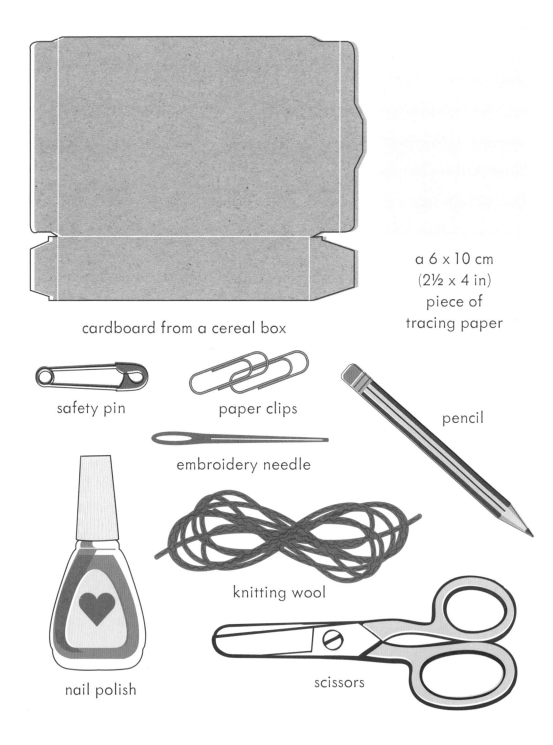

cardboard from a cereal box

a 6 x 10 cm
(2½ x 4 in)
piece of
tracing paper

safety pin

paper clips

pencil

embroidery needle

nail polish

knitting wool

scissors

you will need

a cereal box

some tracing paper

a safety pin

two paper clips

an embroidery needle

a pencil

nail polish

knitting wool

and a pair of scissors

First you need to make a pattern.

Place the edge of your tracing paper
against the dotted line on the page.

Carefully trace the outline on
the page onto the tracing paper.

Cut along the solid lines on
the tracing paper.

Your pattern will have an empty
space in the middle.

place
edge of
tracing
paper
here

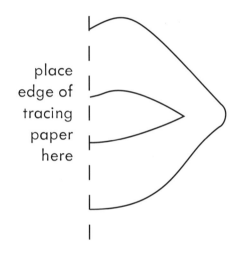

actual-size pattern

Now cut a 12 x 9 cm (5 x 3½ in) piece of cardboard from your cereal box.

Fold it in half.

Place the straight edge of your lips pattern on the folded edge of your card and secure with two paper clips.

Trace around the lips pattern.

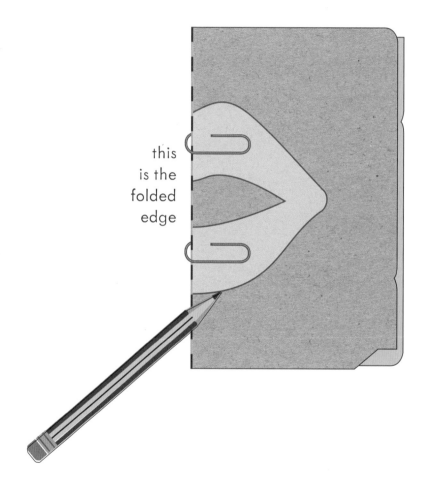

this
is the
folded
edge

Carefully cut out your cardboard template.

Ask an adult to help you cut out the inside part if it is difficult.

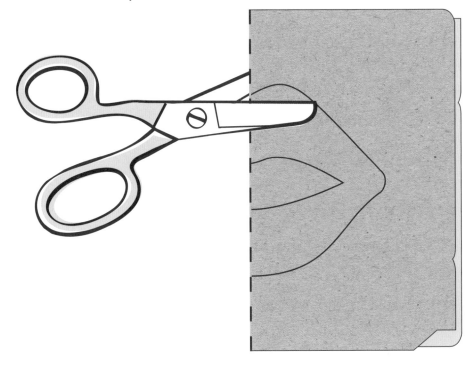

When you unfold the template,
the shape will look like this.

this is the
fold line

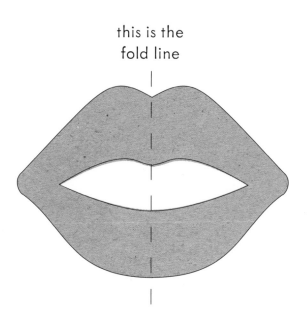

Paint your template with nail polish on one side. This will stop the cardboard color showing through your wool. Let it dry.

front

Cut a very long piece of wool, about 2.5 m (98 in). Thread your embroidery needle with the wool.

Thread one end of your wool through the open mouth and tie it in a double knot in the middle of the top lip. Leave a short loose end.

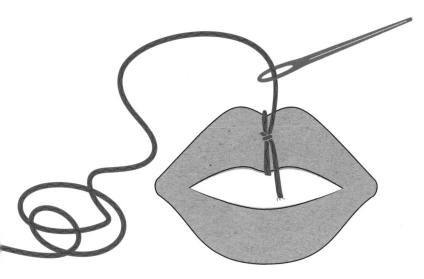

back

Now you are ready to blanket stitch around your brooch.

Hold your template with the knot at the back and the needle pulled up away from the lips.

Bring your needle to the front of the lips and down through the open mouth. Then bring the needle up through the loop you have just made.

Pull your wool firmly upwards until it feels like it locks.

This is your first blanket stitch.

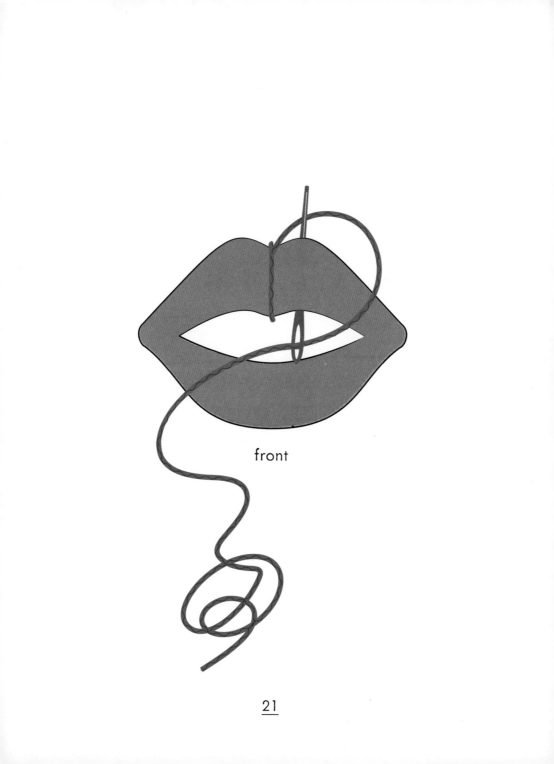

front

Repeat your blanket stitch, working around your lips to create a ridge of stitches along the outside edge.

Remember to pull your needle firmly to make your stitches nice and neat.

When you have stitched all around your template, tie your wool tightly to the loose end of the knot you made at the start.

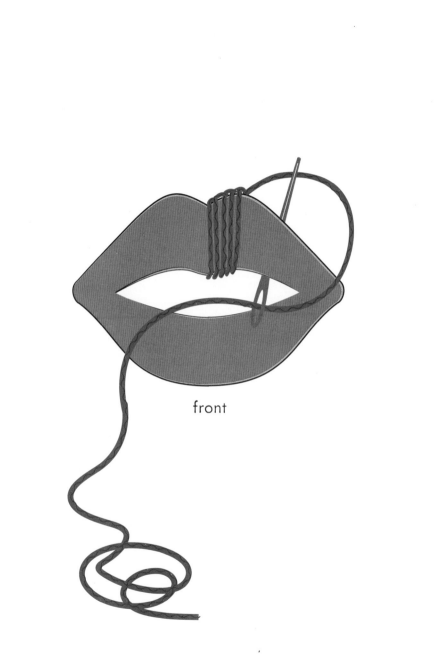

front

Open your safety pin. Carefully slide
the rounded top through a section
of six or seven blanket stitches at
the back of the lips.

Check that you can easily open
and close the safety pin.

back

Your lips brooch is finished.

- -

Go to page 160 for ideas to make more fashion accessories using blanket stitch.

cat ears

15 x 15 cm (6 x 6 in) of felt

a 7 x 7 cm (3 x 3 in)
piece of tracing paper

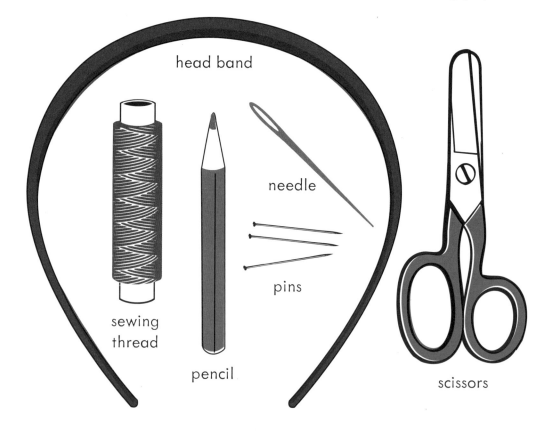

head band

sewing
thread

pencil

needle

pins

scissors

you will need

a piece of felt

some tracing paper

a fabric-covered head band

sewing thread

a pencil

a needle

some pins

and a pair of scissors

First you need to make a pattern for your cat ears.

Fold the tracing paper in half.

Place the folded edge against the dotted line on the page.

Carefully trace the outline on the page onto the tracing paper.

Cut around the solid line on the tracing paper. Don't cut along the folded edge.

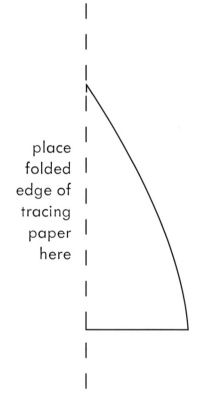

place
folded
edge of
tracing
paper
here

<u>actual-size pattern</u>

When you unfold the pattern,
the shape will look like this.

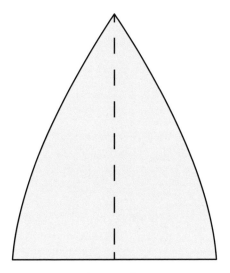

this is the
fold line

Fold your felt in half.

Place the bottom edge of your
pattern on the folded edge of
the felt. Leave enough room for
the second ear.

Pin the pattern to the felt.

Cut around the edge of the pattern.
Don't cut along the folded edge
of the felt.

Take out the pins and repin the
pattern to the leftover felt.
Cut out your second ear.

this is the folded edge

Unfold one ear shape and lay
it on a flat surface. Place your
head band on top of it.

Fold the ear shape in half around the
head band. Line up the edges
of the ear shape and pin the two
layers together.

Now pin on the other ear.

Try on the head band to check
the the ears look right. Be careful
of the pins!

Sew two or three stitches through both the head band fabric and the bottom corner of one ear, to secure the ear in place.

Then sew around the edges of the ear. Make sure you sew through both layers of felt.

When you reach the other bottom corner, sew another two or three stitches through your head band fabric.

Repeat for the second ear.

Your cat ears are finished.

- -

Go to page 169 for ideas to make more fashion accessories with animal ears.

a bag charm

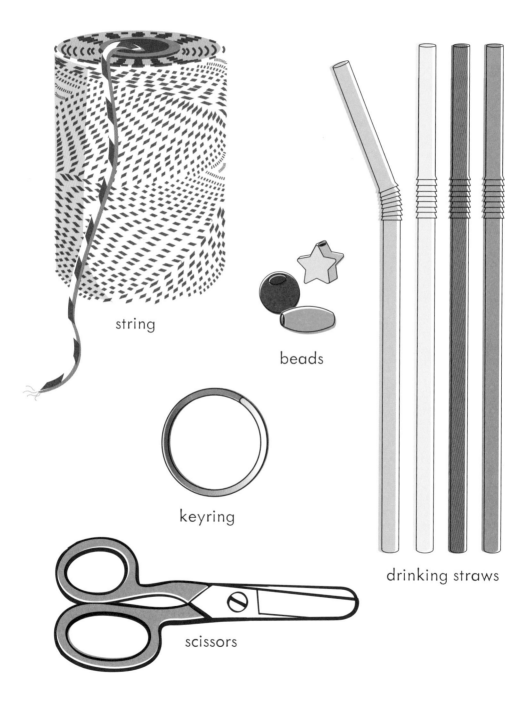

string

beads

keyring

scissors

drinking straws

you will need

some string

some beads

some drinking straws

a keyring

and a pair of scissors

First you need to cut about
15 to 20 strands of string.

Each strand should be about
30 cm (12 in) long.

Thread the strands through
your keyring. Make sure the
ends all line up together.

Cut a long piece of string, about 60 cm (24 in). Wind it tightly round and round the top of your strands.

To finish, tie the end of the long string to one of the strands with a tight double knot.

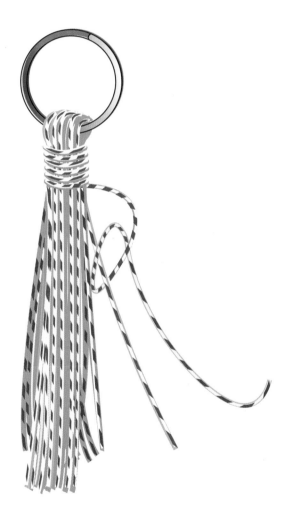

Take a handful of straws and cut
them into lots of small pieces.

Make sure to hold the straws over
a paper or plastic bag as you cut
them, so the pieces of straw don't
fly across the room!

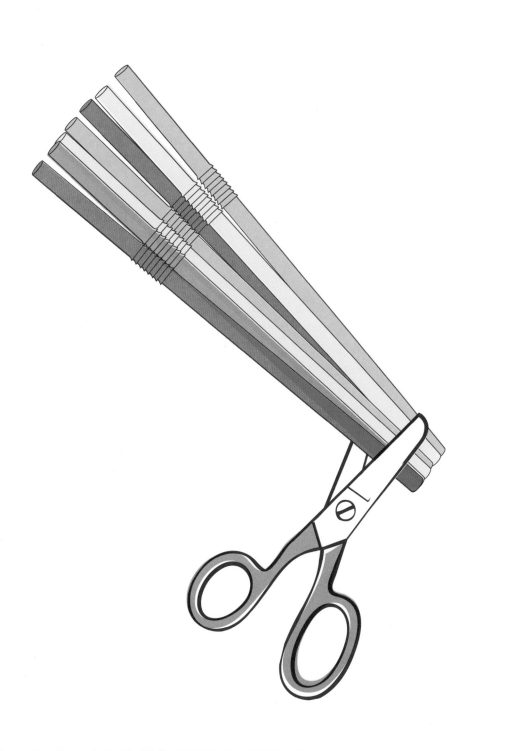

Thread a few straw pieces onto
a strand. Finish off with a bead.

Tie a double knot below the bead.
Make sure the knot is big enough
so the straws and bead don't fall off.
Tie another knot on top if needed.

Snip off the thread ends to make
the knot nice and neat.

Repeat until all the strands are
threaded with straw pieces
and beads.

Your bag charm is finished.

- -

See page 165 for ideas to make
more fashion accessories with tassels.

a festival garland

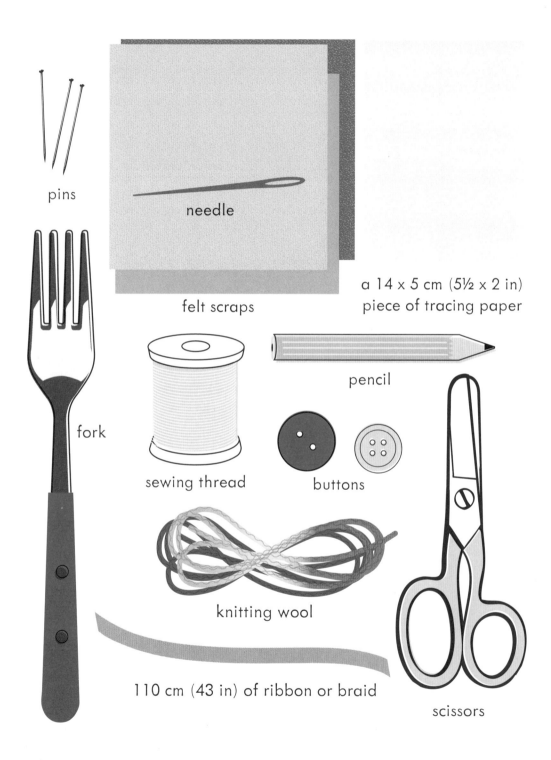

pins

needle

felt scraps

a 14 x 5 cm (5½ x 2 in)
piece of tracing paper

fork

pencil

sewing thread

buttons

knitting wool

110 cm (43 in) of ribbon or braid

scissors

you will need

some pins

a needle

felt scraps

some tracing paper

a fork

sewing thread

a pencil

some buttons

knitting wool

some ribbon or braid

and a pair of scissors

First you need to make a pattern
for the flowers.

Carefully trace the outline on
the page onto the tracing paper.

Cut around the solid line on the
tracing paper to make your pattern.

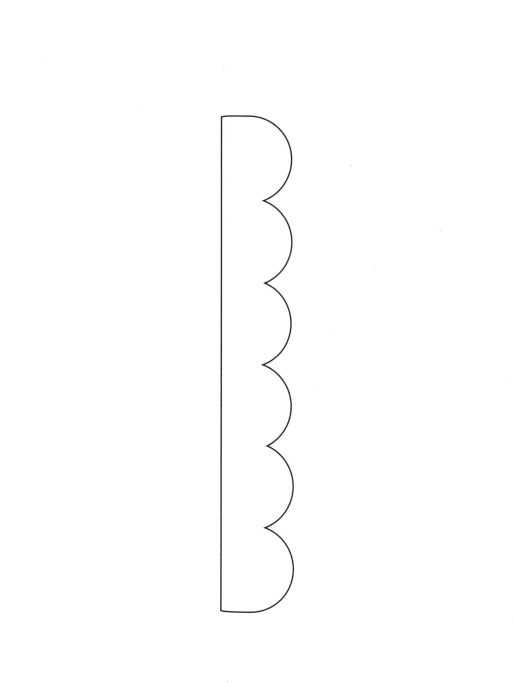

actual-size pattern

Pin the pattern to your felt.

Carefully cut all around
the edge of the pattern.

Then take out the pins
and lift off the pattern.

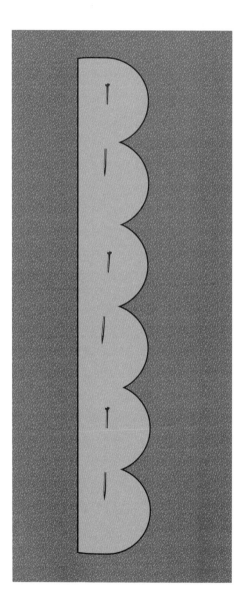

Now you are ready to sew.

Double-thread your needle.
Go to page 170 if you're not
sure how to do this.

Sew along the straight edge
of your felt shape.

Do not cut off your thread
when you reach the end!

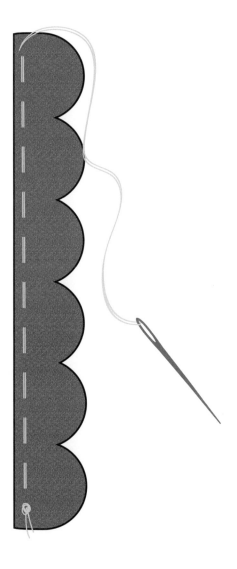

Now gently pull the thread so your felt shape gathers together in the center.

Pull the thread tight and tie a double knot close to the felt.

Do not cut off your thread yet!

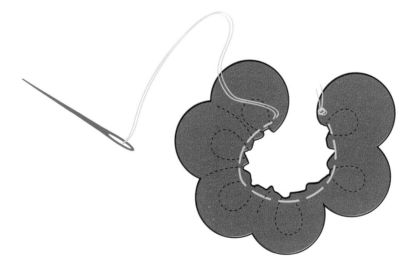

Sew the first and last petals together with two little stitches, close to the center.

Do not cut off your thread yet!

Sew on a button in the center of your flower, still using the same thread.

Make sure to knot your thread on the same side of the flower as the other knots.

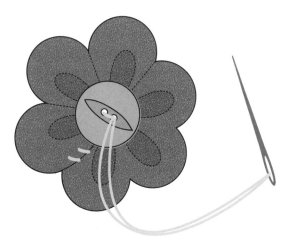

Make some more felt flowers
in different colors.

Now make some pom-poms.

Cut off a length of wool about 20 cm (8 in) long and put it to one side.

Take your ball of wool and wrap one end round the prongs of a fork, about 25 times.

Cut off the wool and hold the end in place on your fork.

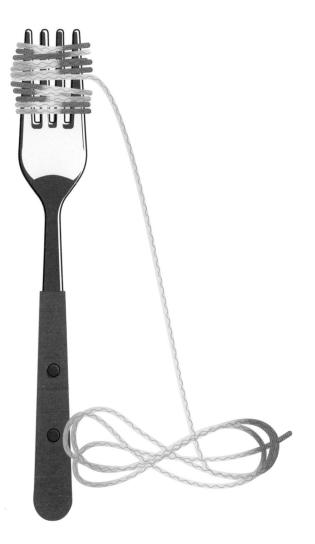

Thread one end of your shorter
piece of wool through the middle
gap between the fork prongs.
Then tie it very tightly around
the middle of the wool loops.

Tie a tight double knot in the
wool so it doesn't come undone.

Slip the little woollen bow
off the fork prongs.

Cut the loops at each end of your
bow shape. Fluff out the strands.

Make some more pom-poms.

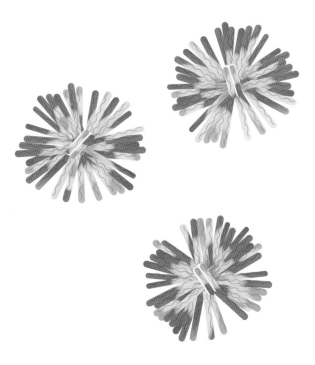

Pin your flowers and pom-poms
to your ribbon or braid, where
you think they will look nice.

Hold the garland up to your head
to check that you're happy with
how it looks. Be careful of the pins!

Then sew on the flowers and the
pom-poms with four or five tight
stitches each. Remember to take
out the pins!

Your festival garland is finished.

Tie it in a bow at the back of
your head.

- -

Go to pages 162 and 163 for ideas
to make more fashion accessories
with felt flowers and pom-poms.

a pasta necklace

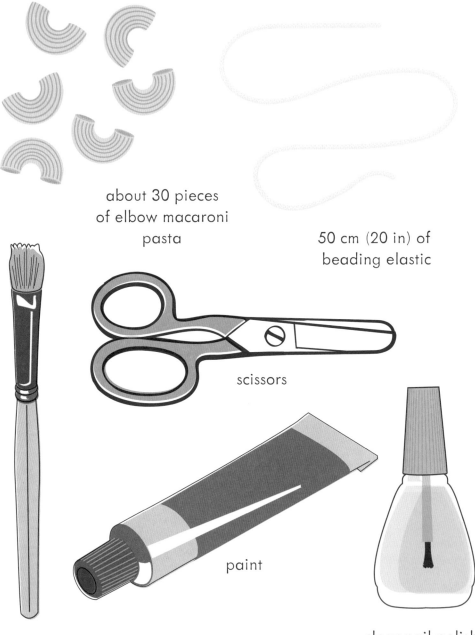

about 30 pieces
of elbow macaroni
pasta

50 cm (20 in) of
beading elastic

scissors

paint

clear nail polish

paintbrush

you will need

some elbow macaroni pasta

some beading elastic

a paintbrush

a pair of scissors

some paint

and clear nail polish

This can be a messy job! Make sure to cover the area where you are working with some old newspapers, and put on an apron so your clothes don't get paint on them!

Lay your pasta out on some newspaper and paint one side of each piece. Let the paint dry.

Turn over your pasta and paint the other side. Let the paint dry.

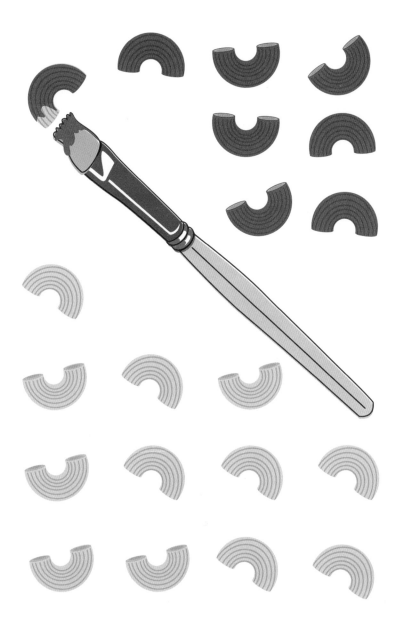

Tie a loose knot about 10 cm (4 in) from one end of your elastic.

Paint some clear nail polish on the other end. Let it dry. This makes the elastic end less fluffy and easier to thread through your pasta pieces.

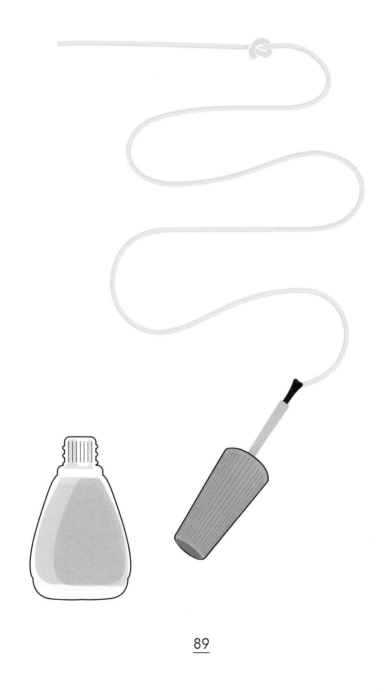

Thread the elastic through one
pasta piece.

Thread on the next piece of
pasta so together they make
a letter S shape.

Thread on another piece so the
pasta starts to look like a wavy line.

Keep going until your necklace
looks about the right length.
Hold it up to your neck to check.

Now tie the ends of the elastic together with a tight double knot.

Snip off the ends.

Your pasta necklace is finished.

- -

Go to page 164 for ideas to make more fashion accessories with pasta shapes.

a braided belt

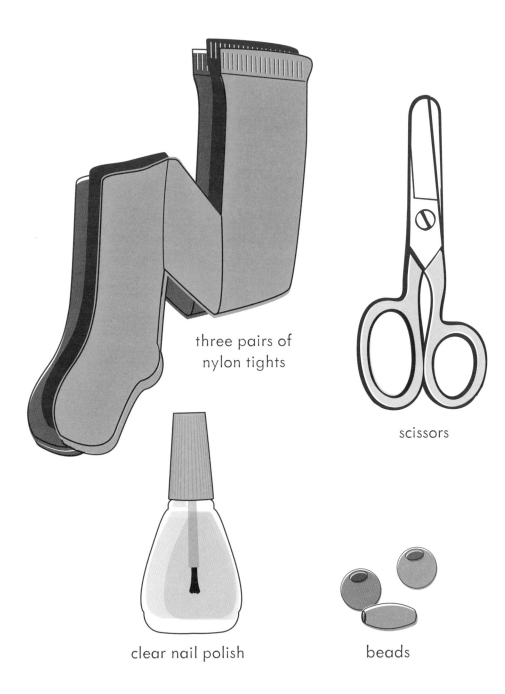

three pairs of
nylon tights

scissors

clear nail polish

beads

you will need

some nylon tights in
different colors or designs

a pair of scissors

clear nail polish

some beads with big holes
in the middle

First you need to cut the toes
off each pair of tights.

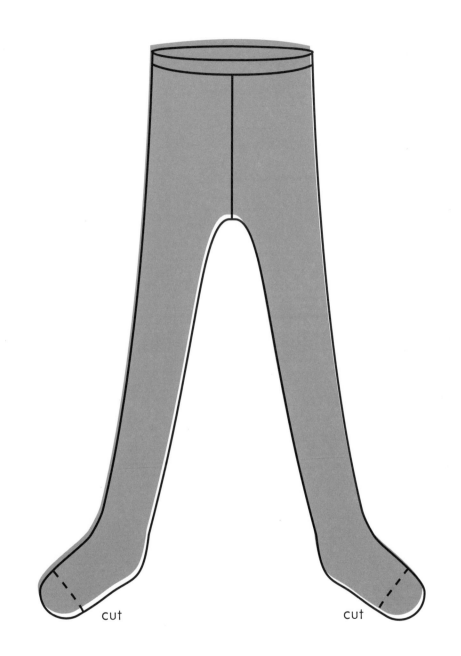

cut

cut

Then cut a strip, about 4 cm (1½ in) wide, out of each pair of tights.

Cut up the inside of one leg, across the gusset, then down the inside of the other leg.

Paint both ends of the strips with a little clear nail polish. Let it dry. This makes the ends less fluffy and easier to thread through beads.

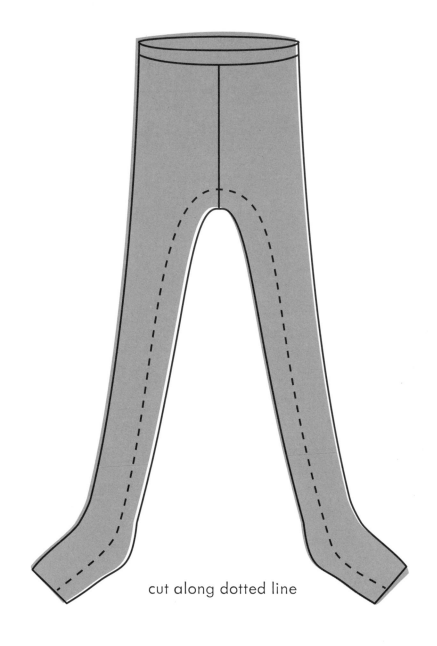

cut along dotted line

Line up the ends of your strips.
Then tie all the strips together
in a big knot, about 20 cm (8 in)
from one end.

Now you are ready to braid.

The strips will be very long, so hold
them in place by loosely tying the ends
nearest to the knot to a door handle.
This will make them easier to braid.

Make sure to use a door that won't
be opened while you are braiding!

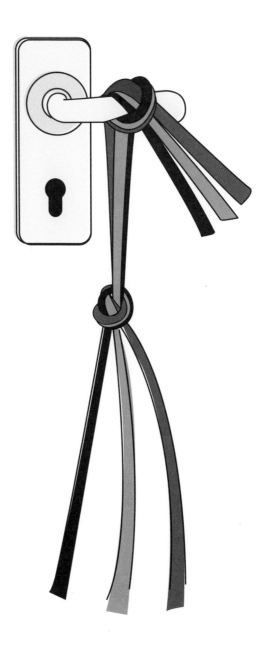

1. Take the strip on the left and pass it over the middle one. This strip is now in the middle.

2. Take the strip on the right and pass it over the middle one. This strip is now in the middle.

3. Again, take the strip on the left and pass it over the middle one.

4. And again, take the strip on the right and pass it over the middle one.

Keep going until you are about 20 cm (8 in) from the end.

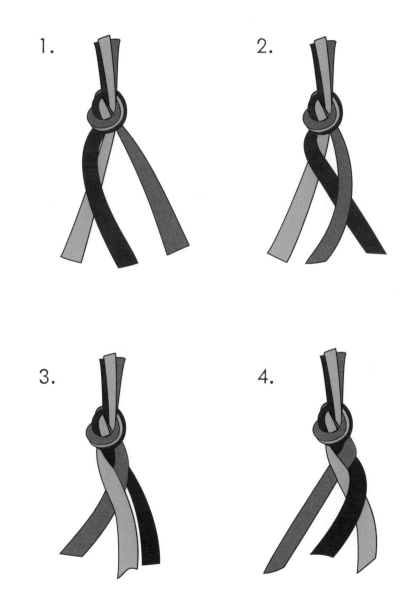

1.

2.

3.

4.

Tie all the strips in a big knot.

Now untie your braided belt
from the door handle.

Cut the end of each strip into three thinner strips, about 1 cm (½ in) wide.

Thread a bead onto the end of each strip.

Tie a double knot below each bead. Make sure the knot is big enough so the bead doesn't fall off. Tie another knot on top if needed.

Your braided belt is finished.

- -

Go to page 166 for more ideas to make braided fashion accessories.

a jeweled collar

a 20 x 20 cm (8 x 8 in) piece
of tracing paper

30 x 30 cm (12 x 12 in) of felt

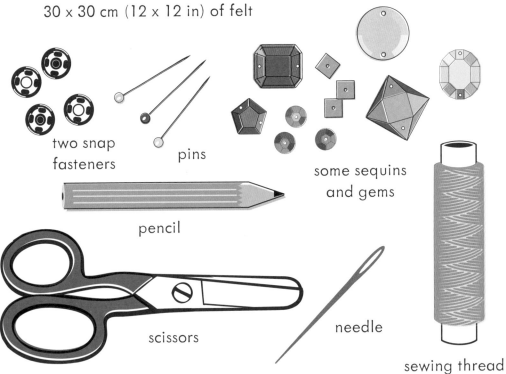

two snap
fasteners

pins

some sequins
and gems

pencil

scissors

needle

sewing thread

you will need

a piece of felt

some tracing paper

two snap fasteners

some pins

some sequins and gems

a pencil

a pair of scissors

a needle

and sewing thread

First you need to make a pattern.

Carefully trace the outline on
the page onto the tracing paper.

Cut around the line on the
tracing paper.

Repeat this to make two
paper patterns.

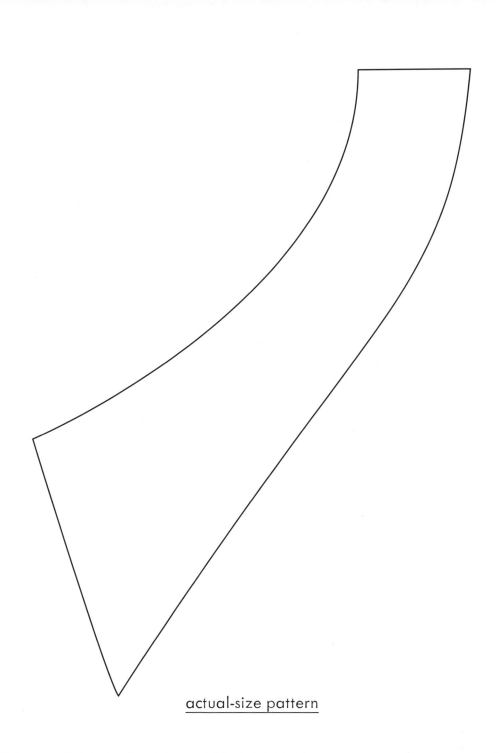

actual-size pattern

Pin the two patterns to your
felt square like this.

This will leave enough felt for
your neckband. The dotted line
shows where to cut the neckband.

Cut all around the edge
of the paper patterns.

Take out the pins and lift
the patterns off the felt.

Now carefully cut your neckband.
It should be about 41 cm (16 in)
long and about 1 cm (½ in) wide.

Fold the neckband in half to find the center. Mark it with a pin.

This will be the front of your collar.

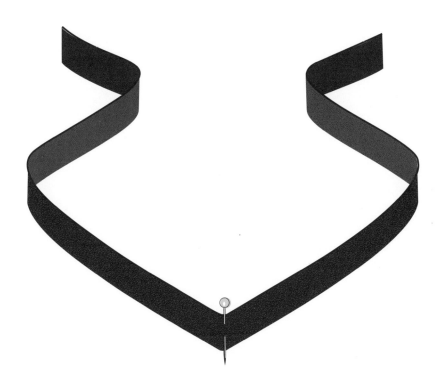

Now lie your neckband flat on
a hard surface.

Line up the top inside corner of one
of the collar shapes with the pin
marking the center of the neckband.

Pin the top edge of the collar shape
along the top edge of the neckband.

Repeat with the second collar shape.

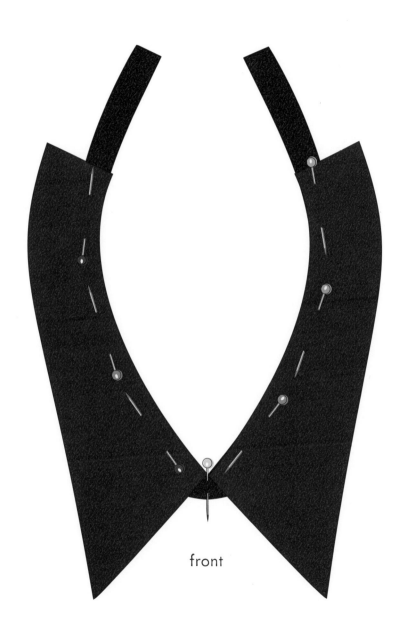

front

125

Sew the collar shapes to the neckband, along the top edge.

Make sure the top edges of the neckband and the collar shapes stay lined up as you sew.

Keep your stitches small and neat.

front

Turn over your collar.

Use the scissors to make small
snips along the bottom edge
of the neckband.

Snip about halfway up the width
of the neckband each time.

Be careful not to cut any of your
stitches, and don't snip too close
to the center of your neckband.

These snips help the neckband to
lie flat against your neck. They are
hidden under the collar shapes
so you can't see them.

back

Sew two snap fasteners onto your neckband, one right at the end and one further towards the collar shapes.

This means you can adjust how high or low the collar sits on your neck.

Make sure the snap fasteners can snap together without twisting your neckband.

Sew on some gems and sequins to decorate your collar.

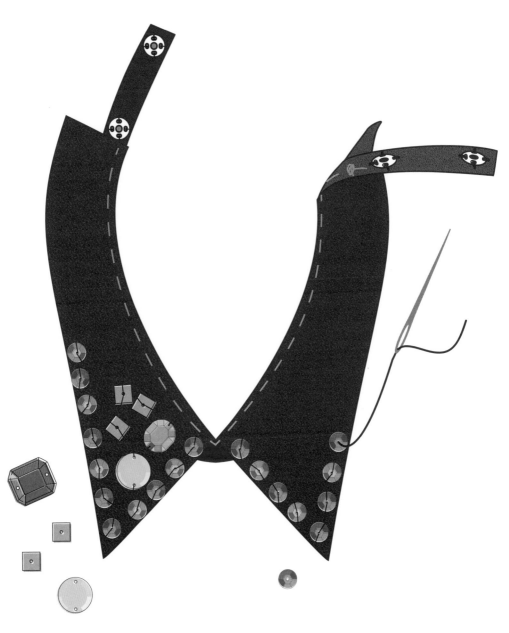

Your jeweled collar is finished.

- -

Go to page 168 for ideas to make more fashion accessories with sequins and other decorations.

a kawaii bear bag

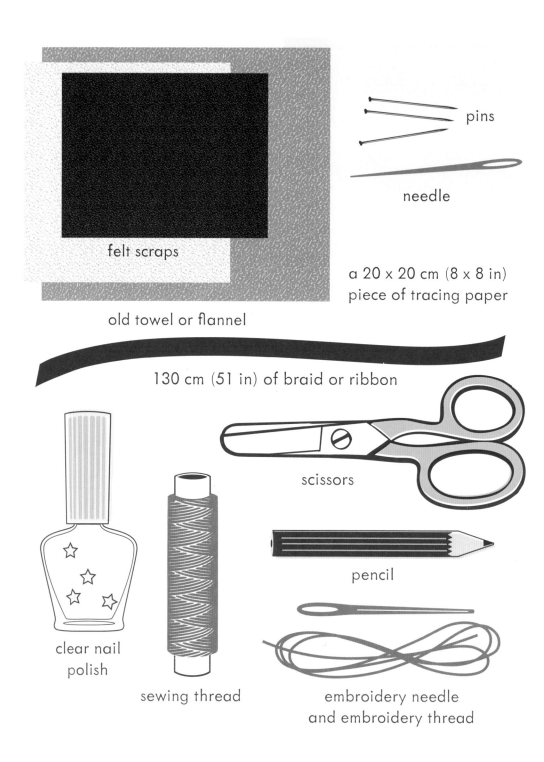

felt scraps

old towel or flannel

pins

needle

a 20 x 20 cm (8 x 8 in) piece of tracing paper

130 cm (51 in) of braid or ribbon

scissors

clear nail polish

sewing thread

pencil

embroidery needle and embroidery thread

you will need

some felt scraps

an old towel or flannel

some pins

a needle

some tracing paper

some braid or ribbon

a pair of scissors

clear nail polish

sewing thread

a pencil

an embroidery needle

some embroidery thread

First you need to make a pattern.

Fold the tracing paper in half.

Carefully trace the outline on
the page onto the tracing paper.

Cut around the solid line on the
tracing paper. Don't cut along
the folded edge.

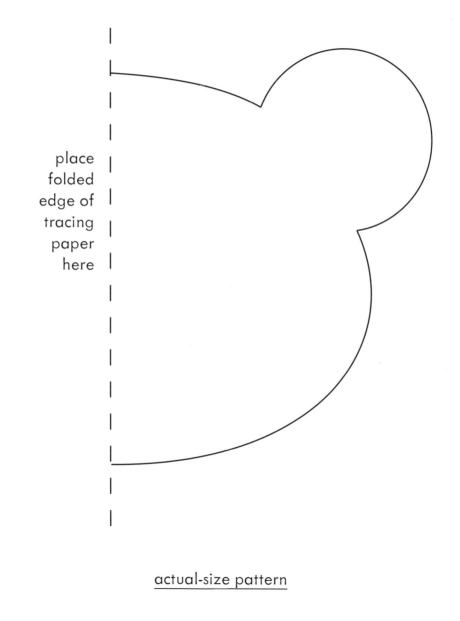

place
folded
edge of
tracing
paper
here

actual-size pattern

When you unfold the pattern,
the shape will look like this.

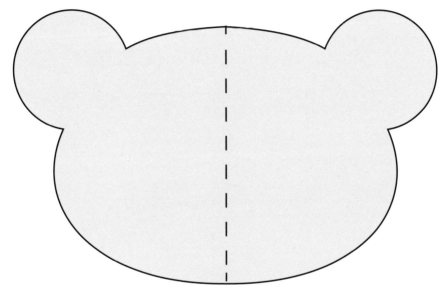

this is the
fold line

Now make the patterns for your bear's face.

Carefully trace the outlines on the page onto the leftover tracing paper.

Cut out the shapes.

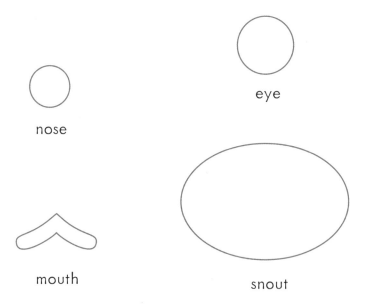

nose

eye

mouth

snout

actual-size patterns

Pin the patterns to your pieces
of felt. The snout needs to be
a different color to the rest.

Cut all around the edges of the
patterns. Cut out two eyes.

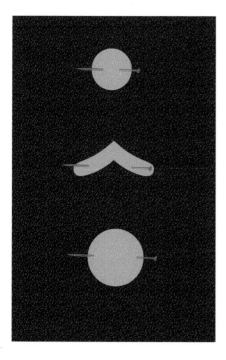

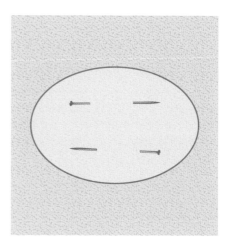

Now fold your towel in half,
fluffy sides together.

Pin the head pattern to the towel.

Cut all around the edge of the
pattern. Make sure you cut
through both layers of fabric.

Take out the pins and lift
the pattern off the towel.

Paint clear nail polish along
the edge of the towel shapes.
Let them dry. This stops the fabric
from fraying and looking messy.

this is the folded edge

Now you are ready to sew on your bear's face. The technique you will use is called appliqué.

Sew the nose and mouth onto the snout, using small stitches.

Then pin the snout onto the head shape. Pin on the eyes either side of it.

Sew on the snout and eyes, using small stitches.

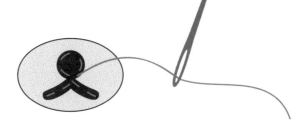

front piece

Lay the back piece of your bag,
the piece without the face, fluffy
side down on a flat surface.

Tie a knot at each end of the ribbon.

Pin one ribbon end to each ear.
Make sure the ribbon lies flat
and doesn't twist.

Sew down the ribbon ends with
three or four stitches.

back piece
(inside)

Pin the two pieces of your bag together. Make sure the ribbon knots are on the inside and your bear's face is on the outside!

Now you are ready to blanket stitch your bag together.

Thread your embroidery needle with your embroidery thread and knot it at the end.

1.

2.

Repeat your blanket stitch, working around your bear's head. Pull your needle firmly, but not too tight, so your stitches are nice and neat.

Remember to leave an opening at the top of your bear's head, between the ears.

Do not cut off your thread yet!

Now blanket stitch across the top of the front piece, the one with your bear's face.

Make sure to stitch through only one layer so you don't close up the opening.

Then blanket stitch across the top of the back piece.

Poke your needle back through to the inside of your bag. Tie two or three tight knots close to the fabric.

Your kawaii bear bag is finished.

Go to page 167 for ideas to make more fashion accessories using appliqué.

let's design ...

Now you have learned to use the techniques in this book, you can design and create your own fashion accessories.

Start by making your own brooches and bracelets and soon you will be designing your own bag! Here are a few ideas to get you started.

with blanket stitch (pages 9 and 135)

1. Make a bunny-shaped template and use super-fluffy wool to make bunnies.

2. Make shapes with bendy wire and cover them with blanket stitch, then make them into brooches and necklaces.

3. Blanket stitch around an old bangle. Tie short pieces of different colored threads together and leave the ends to make little tassels.

4. Blanket stitch a pair of flip flops and add pom-poms.

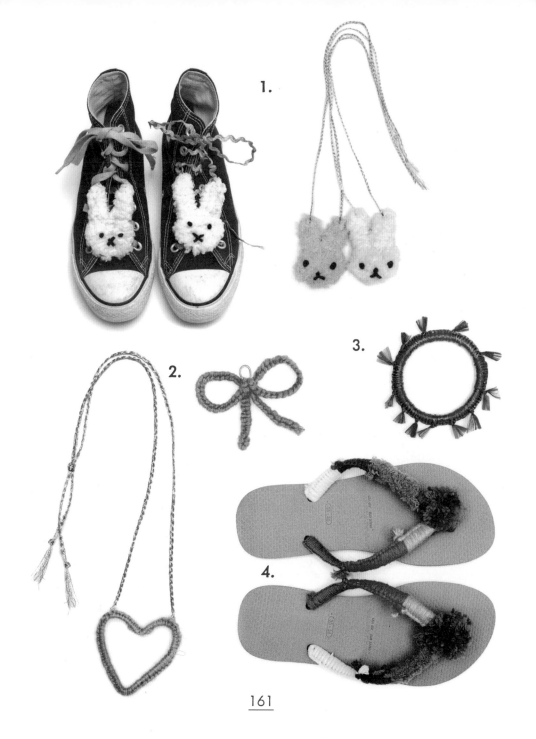

1.

2.

3.

4.

with pom-poms (page 72)

1. Sew pom-poms onto socks and hair bands.

2. Add felt leaves to your pom-poms to make a cherry brooch.

3. Add a felt face to a pom-pom for a cute bag charm.

1.

2.

3.

with felt flowers (page 62)

1. Glue flowers onto sunglasses and hair clips.

2. Make a flower into a brooch by sewing a safety pin onto the back.

1.

2.

with pasta shapes (page 83)

1. Decorate pasta bows with paint and glitter, then glue them to hair clips.

2. Use different types of pasta to make bracelets and necklaces.

with tassels (page 45)

1. Color the ends of a string tassel with felt-tip pens to give a dip-dye effect.

2. Try chunky beads and bright string, or use gold beads to add some bling! Use your tassel as a keyring, or thread a belt through it to make it into a belt charm.

1.

2.

with braiding (page 97)

1. Cut strips from an old pair of jeans to make a 70s-look braided belt.

2. Use nylon tights to make a stylish braided wristband.

3. Braid some wool to make a chain for a key necklace, or a colorful hairpiece knotted onto a hair tie.

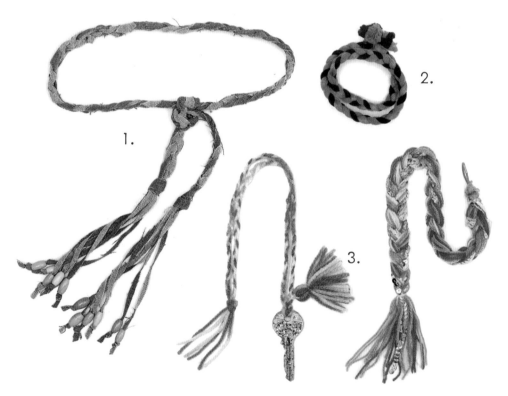

with appliqué (page 135)

1. Make a bunny or cat template for more cute bags.

2. Cut out fun felt shapes and sew them onto a purse, a T-shirt or a pair of jeans.

1.

2.

with buttons, sequins and beads
(pages 130 and 174)

1. Cover felt shapes with sequins to make sew-on patches for your clothes or your bag.

2. Splatter paint over buttons and glue them to hair clips.

3. Sew sequins and buttons onto socks. Make sure to sew them on separately so the socks can still stretch when you put them on.

1.

2.

3.

with animal ears (page 29)

1. Make mouse ears by cutting out felt circle shapes.

2. Use faux-fur to make tiger ears.

3. Tie a long, thick piece of felt into a knot and cut the ends into bunny ear shapes.

1.

2.

3.

tips and techniques

threading your needle

1. Cut off about 45 cm (18 in) of your sewing thread. Thread one end through the hole in your needle. Tie a double knot at that end (see opposite).

2. Snip off the thread ends, close to the knot. Leave the other end of the thread hanging loose on one side of the needle.

double-threading your needle

Double-threading makes your stitches stronger.

1. Cut off about 90 cm (35 in) of sewing thread. Thread one end through the hole in your needle.

2. Tie the ends of the thread together in a double knot (see opposite). Snip off the thread ends, close to the knot.

tying knots

overhand knot

1. Make a loop, crossing one end of the thread over the other.

2. Pass one thread end through the loop you've just made.

3. Pull both ends to tighten your knot.

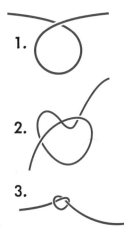

double knot

1. Tie two overhand knots, one on top of the other.

2. Carefully pull both ends to tighten the knot. Make sure one loop doesn't close before the other.

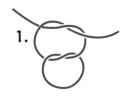

knotting tips

Try to tie your knot on the wrong side of your work so it doesn't show. Snip off the thread ends close to the knot, to keep it neat.

running stitch

1. Poke the needle up through the fabric. Gently pull until the knot stops the thread. Sew two stitches on top of each other.

2. Now start your running stitch. Make each stitch by pushing the needle down through both layers of fabric and then back up again a little further along. Make your stitches quite small and all the same size.

3. To finish, sew two stitches on top of each other. See opposite for how to tie a special knot through these two stitches.

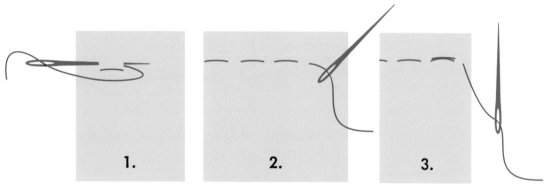

1.   2.   3.

cast-off knot

Once you have sewn two stitches on top of each other at the end of your running stitch, you can tie a special knot to finish.

1. Bring your needle back up through your fabric, close to the last two stitches. Slip your needle under these stitches to make a loop.

2. Now pass your needle back through the loop you have just made. Pull the thread tightly to make a knot.

Repeat two or three times to make sure the knot is secure, so your stitches don't come undone. Snip off the thread ends, close to the knot.

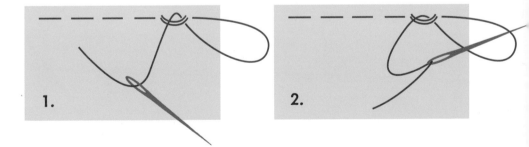

sewing on buttons, sequins and gems

1. Knot the end of your double thread. Hold the button against the fabric. Push the needle up through the fabric and through one of the holes in the button. Pull the thread so the knot is tight against the fabric.

2. Sew back down through a different hole in the button. Repeat the stitch two or three times. To finish, knot the thread on the wrong side of the fabric.

To sew on a sequin or gem, follow the steps above but sew through the holes as shown below.

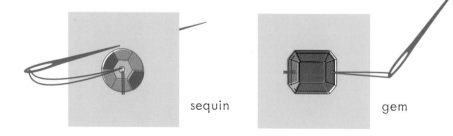

sequin   gem

sewing on snap fasteners

A snap fastener has two halves that snap together. Make sure each one is in the right place and is the right way up before you start sewing.

1. Make two stitches through the fabric where you want to sew on your snap fastener. Then poke your threaded needle up through a hole in the snap fastener.

2. Bring the needle back down through the fabric at the outside edge of the snap fastener.

3. Sew two or three stitches through each hole in the snap fastener. To finish, knot your thread at the back.

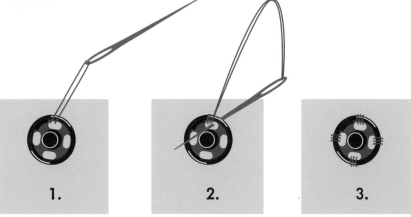

1.   2.   3.

First published in the United Kingdom in 2016 by Thames & Hudson Ltd,
181A High Holborn, London WC1V 7QX

I Can Make My Own Accessories © 2016 Thames & Hudson Ltd, London

All photographs by Pascal Bergamin

All the accessories featured in this book are the original works of the authors.

Created by Louise Scott-Smith and Georgia Vaux
Fashion design by Louise Scott-Smith
Graphic design by Georgia Vaux
Model: Bobby Sandbach

First published in 2016 in hardcover in the United States of America
by Thames & Hudson Inc., 500 Fifth Avenue, New York, New York 10110

thamesandhudsonusa.com

Library of Congress Catalog Card Number 2016931312

ISBN 978-0-500-65082-0

Printed and bound in China by Everbest Printing Co. Ltd

To find out about all our publications,
please visit **www.thamesandhudson.com**
There you can subscribe to our e-newsletter,
browse or download our current catalogue,
and buy any titles that are in print.